VOLUME 1

30 Tips To Unlock Your Potential

BEN GLENN

BUILDING SUCCESS

BRICK by BRICK

Building Success Brick By Brick, Volume 1

Cover design by Cara Tudor

Library of Congress Cataloging-in-Publication Data

Glenn, Ben
Building Success Brick by Brick, Volume 1 / Ben Glenn
p. cm.
Includes biographic reference
ISBN 978-0-9675680-2-7 (paperback)
1. Teen Issues
2. Inspiration
3. Self Help

I. Glenn, Ben II. Title

Library of Congress Catalog Card Number: 2012951504

TABLE OF CONTENTS

TABLE OF CONTENTS (continued)

TABLE OF CONTENTS (continued)

Introduction

BUILDING SUCCESS

Seven Ways To Achieve Your Potential with Plastic Toy Bricks

"Play is our brain's favorite way of learning."
– Diane Ackerman

When I was a kid, I spent hours at a time in a pile of LEGO building bricks, constructing cars, boats, planes, and spaceships. It was my own little world made out of thousands of interlocking pieces. I was crazy about LEGOs. Forget swimming in a pit of plastic balls; fill it with LEGOs and let me dive right in! (On second thought, ouch.)

Honestly, I still love LEGOs, and I'll pick up a cool-looking set from time to time. I recently realized that LEGOs can do more than let me build whatever my imagination comes up with. They can teach me to build myself up to be the kind of person that I want to be.

Once I started thinking about it, the parallels between building colorful toy spaceships and building a successful life snapped together. I don't know if I can think of a more playful teaching tool to encourage you to achieve focus, stay on track, and move forward in life. So, with LEGOs on the brain, I'd like to share my observations and things I've learned over the last 20 years spent speaking, drawing, and just trying to live the best life I can.

While reading this, I recommend that you grab a few LEGOs to play with. It'll be a fun way to remember that success isn't something you're born with, and it doesn't happen overnight. You build it, brick by brick.

Plates : Finding the foundation for success

"Deep meaning lies often in childish play." – Johann Friedrich von Schiller, German poet

Let's say that you've got your LEGO set out, and you want a build a big apple – even better, how about THE Big Apple, New York City? You'll start with plates. Plates are the foundation for your model, and they determine what you can build, how big you can build it, and how sturdy it will be. The same is true when building a successful life; you need to start with a strong foundation.

With LEGOs, you typically begin with the largest plate as the core foundation, and then smaller plates are added. This large plate is the most important piece of the model because everything builds upon it. It provides stability and structure.

To be successful, you also need a core foundation to build your life upon. My core is the plate of attitude, which is how I think or feel. Attitude is fundamental it provides stability and structure to how I behave in every situation.

Upon attitude, I attach the plate of faith, a belief in myself, God, and others. Then I add optimism, working to always think positive. Finally, I attach vision, which is thinking big, dreaming big, and working to keep success in sight.

With all of my plates in place, I have a solid foundation, and that's the crucial first step to building success!

Bricks: The Construction of Character

Once the plates are in place, it's time to attach bricks. Bricks come in a variety of shapes and sizes. You can choose to arrange them in one of countless ways. When building a successful life, character qualities are your bricks, and you can choose what qualities define your character, which is what makes you a unique individual. So, you're sitting with a heaping pile of LEGOs of all different kinds. How do you know which bricks to choose? You consult your vision for the model - the picture in your mind of what you want to build. For now, let's stay with New York City. If you want to build the Empire State Building, you'll probably pick a lot of gray bricks with blue or white bricks for windows. For the Statue of Liberty, you might go with green with some yellow for her torch.

Your vision for a successful life - your goals and dreams - will guide which character qualities you choose. For example, if your vision for success says that you should be humble, then you should select a brick of Humility and stack it on your foundation. Picking a brick of Bragging wouldn't fit in your vision; leave that one in the pile.

When people fail to consult their vision, they just take on character qualities at random. That leads nowhere near success. If you've stacked LEGO bricks with no plan, you know that it leads to an unstable and unidentifiable mess.

Think before you pick, and success will start to take form!

2 KEY QUESTIONS:

- **What is your vision of success?**
- **What are the qualities you need to achieve that vision of success?**

Pieces in Pairs: Keeping Your Balance.

When you pour a new box of LEGOs out on the table, you'll notice that pieces typically come in even numbers: two windows, four wheels, eight plates, and so on. This is to give the model balance. If you're building a car and you only have three wheels, one corner of the car can drag. In the same way, a successful life needs balance.

For example, if you choose a brick of strength, then you should add a brick of humility to balance it out. Note that strength and humility aren't opposites, but they complement each other. A strong person should be humble so that they don't become boastful with their strength. Or if you choose humor, then balance it with sensitivity to keep your jokes from offending or hurting people.

Without balance, our model for success will have good qualities that go too far. Confident people might become conceited. Funny people could turn obnoxious. And just like a model plane with only one wing, the whole thing falls over.

Keep your balance and keep building!

Opportunities: Your Definition of Success May Change

I've loved LEGOs since I was a kid, and they just keep getting better! New kinds of bricks come out all the time. My imagination is stretched by the ever-evolving possibilities of what I can build. A successful life keeps up with changes and new opportunities, too.

LEGOs evolve in all sorts of ways: new colors, bricks that move in new ways, and new sets. There's a Space Shuttle set now, but there wasn't when LEGOs started in the 1940s – because there wasn't a Space Shuttle in the 1940s! And good luck finding a Harry Potter set from the '80s! (Harry's first book came out in '97.)

As you build your successful life, watch for new opportunities. Maybe you'll try playing the guitar and realize that you like it. So, you might add musician to your definition of the person you want to be. Or perhaps you'll move to Colorado and fall in love with rock climbing. Or wouldn't it be cool if you enrolled into that wizard school that opened up down the street? (The last Harry Potter reference, I promise!) You never know what fun and exciting opportunity lies around the corner, so keep watching!

Rebuilding: Don't Be Afraid to Start Over

When building a LEGO model, sometimes you'll find that there's a better way to piece things together than you first thought. It's not that there was a problem with your original vision; you just can't predict every trouble spot before it comes up. Your best option is to break it apart and rebuild. A model for success can benefit from rebuilding, too.

Maybe your car model would look better in red than in blue. Or your Empire State Building leans a lot like that famous tower in Pisa. Recently, I had a decent airplane in the works until I realized that it just wasn't going to turn out the way I planned. I took it apart, and now I have a Noah's Ark that floats my boat.

A successful life takes note of what's not working. If you're trying to exercise, you might realize that you just don't enjoy running. So, you try swimming instead. Maybe you realized that your college major isn't some thing that you'd actually like to do. Or you may really want to be Champion of the Westminster Dog Show, but you're not a dog.

Starting over might feel like failure, but you're actually learning that there's a better way to reach your goal. And learning is a good thing.

There's more than one way to success, so feel free to rebuild!

Perseverance: Success Keeps Moving

If you walk through the LEGO section at the store, you'll notice that most of the models are vehicles: cars, trains, planes, and more. First you build it and then you move it; some models even move themselves! Your model of success needs to keep moving, too, especially when it feels like life is stuck at a standstill.

When I was a kid, there were many times when I wanted to throw a LEGO model against a wall – not because I was building a LEGO tennis ball, but because I was frustrated that I couldn't get it to turn out the way I wanted. However, I'm glad that I didn't give in to frustration, because I would have missed out on creating some very cool models.

In a successful life, perseverance is the act of pushing through when you could just give up out of frustration or anger. In the face of challenge, you dig deep and tap into your inner motivation, discipline, and self-control. This could be finishing a tough project for school or working through a rough patch in your marriage.

I love how Bill Hybels said, "Most people quit when the finish line is just right around the corner."

Keep moving forward and you'll reach the finish line eventually. You'll be glad that you did!

Play: A Celebration

What's my motivation for building with LEGOs? It's FUN! I love envisioning a model in my mind and then actually creating it with my cherished plastic toy bricks. It can be hard work, but it gives me a sense of accomplishment and satisfaction. And when I was younger, I took my new creations and played with them for hours.
As we get older, we forget the benefits that

come from playing. We get so wrapped up in work, money, and status that forget to celebrate with play. Play is a time to rest from your work and enjoy life. It can also be a time to open your mind to new visions and find a spark of motivation for the next challenge.

A successful life needs play. Enjoy your success Rejoice in your journey and all that you've built, all that you've learned and all that you've become.

There will always be building to be done, so you might as well play on a regular basis!

"You cannot dream yourself into a character; you must hammer and forge yourself one."
– Henry David Thoreau

Building with LEGOs is a process, and I love that. You pull them out of the box, and you have to work before you can play. With most toys, the only work you have to do is snip off 100 twist-ties (which is no easy task). LEGO models need to be built, and that takes hours. A successful life also needs to be built, and that takes years. The real difference is that the reward of success lasts a lifetime.

When I open a LEGO model, I lay out all of the

pieces first, so when it comes time to add a brick, I don't have to search for it. I can get right to building. In life, many people spend too much time searching for the right pieces to add into their lives instead of actually building better lives. I want to help people stop searching and start building, so I've written this book series.

The Success Building Series is an encouraging, ADHD-friendly resource for your personal building project. My motto is "Keep It Simple!" so each book in the series is less than 100 pages, and yet jam-packed with 30 tips - one tip for each day of the month. The tips are bite-sized, and they'll playfully spark ideas and actions to help you build a better you. Phase One focuses on the foundational areas in our life, and each following Phase will build upon that foundation.

For those of you who struggle with focus (like me), you can watch these tips on You-Tube, in addition to reading them in the books.

I hope that these books will help you achieve your potential and reach success.

Enjoy Building!

Post your LEGO creation at

simplybenglenn

to win FREE stuff!

Success Building Tip 

ATTITUDE, PART 1: THE FOUNDATION

When I was a kid, my mom used to tell me, “Ben, change your attitude!” I was a good kid, but I could never do it – probably because she never explained to me what an attitude was! (I might’ve thought she said “Change your altitude!” and I’d squat down and ask, “Is this enough?”)

It took me a couple of years, or decades, but I finally feel like I have a good understanding of what an attitude is. To have a successful life, it’s essential to understand attitude. So, I’m writing this to help you have a successful life and save you from confusing conversations with your mom.

I define attitude as a consistent way of thinking or feeling, typically reflected in a person’s behavior. In other words, it’s how we normally think or feel about things, and that comes out in how we act. This is why attitude is so important: it determines what we say, what we do, what we don’t do – just about all of the decisions, big or small, that we make. Every waking moment of our lives is rooted in our attitude.

For example, if you wake up to a sunny morning, your attitude can guide you to feeling happy about what a wonderful day it's going to be. Or if someone insults you, your attitude will determine whether you simply walk away (recommended) or if you snap back at them like a rattlesnake (not recommended!). Your attitude will even affect how you feel about this book - happy, I hope! - and how much you learn from it.

Attitude is the most fundamental part of a successful life. And even though it took a while, I just have to say, "Thanks for the advice, Mom!"

TIP: Pay close attention to your thoughts and feelings.

Success Building Tip 2

ATTITUDE, PART 2: POSITIVE/NEGATIVE

Attitude is like food; it comes in all different kinds. Like fruits and vegetables, some kinds of attitude are good for you. Like double-deep-fried peanut butter-filled Twinkies, some are bad for you. For the most part, you can label attitudes as "positive" and "negative."

One example of a positive attitude is cheerfulness, being in a good mood and pleasant to be around. Another is optimism, which is looking for the good side in situations and people. Positive attitudes are valuable gifts that can improve your life and the lives of those around you. But like some valuable gifts, they can be hard to find. Honestly, I'm baffled by how some people can be so optimistic! Do you have to watch Pollyanna 10 times in a row before becoming an optimistic person?

Negative attitudes hurt you and the people in your life. Sarcasm is a type of negative attitude where you use mocking language to hurt someone. Pessimism is the opposite of optimism, so you're expecting the worst in people and situations. And you know what can really leave a bitter taste in your mouth? Bitterness! That's a type of anger or resentment toward something that happened to you (or you think happened to you).

Sometimes, it can be difficult to define an attitude as positive or negative. It might fall into a gray area. But if you're honest with yourself, you can usually tell if an attitude is good or bad for you.

Help yourself to heaping servings of cheerfulness, optimism, and good stuff like that, because a double-deep-fried Twinkie doesn't sound very appetizing (even with peanut butter!)

TIP: Ask yourself if you have a positive or negative attitude.

Success Building Tip 3

ATTITUDE, PART 3: CONTROL

Attitude is so important in life, and the great thing is that you have complete control over it. Just look at the one of the greatest heroes of the 20th century: Buzz Lightyear!

When we first met Buzz, he was a happy-go-lucky space ranger who didn't have a care in the world. Then he found out he was a toy, and his world came crashing down. His fellow toy Woody gives him a pep talk to help him out of his funk, but it's still Buzz's choice to make: go on thinking that he's worthless, or acknowledge that he has significance in the world. At the last moment, Buzz goes with the positive attitude, and he lives a happy life to infinity and beyond... or at least until Toy Story 2.

Even when life throws crazy circumstances your way, you get the final decision on what kind of attitude you adopt. Attitude doesn't happen by accident; it's a choice that you make. And that choice can make all of the difference in the course of your life.

Here's what one of the greatest heroes of the 19th century said about it: "Nothing can stop the man with the right mental attitude from achieving his goal; nothing on earth can help the man with the wrong mental attitude."

That was Thomas Jefferson, author of the Declaration of Independence. What if he adopted an attitude of pessimism back when the 13 colonies were trying to break away from England? The world might be a very different place, and you'd be putting crumpets in your toaster for breakfast instead of Pop Tarts. (And I don't want to imagine a world without Strawberry Pop Tarts!)

In your life, you might find out that your friend got the spot on the basketball team or the car or the job offer that you wanted.
You have the choice to be happy for your friend or to be jealous and spiteful. How you decide will probably affect the course of your friendship.

TIP: Remember that your attitude is your choice, and that you can choose for the best – even if you find out that you're a toy!

Success Building Tip

THE SECRET TO SUCCESS

In stand-up comedy, it's a rare gift to find someone who's hilarious, but also clean. It's not that most comedians don't take showers (actually...) I mean clean, like they tell clean jokes.

That's why I love Ken Davis. He's like the Godfather of Clean Comedy, and he's a hero of mine. I was blessed to spend some time with Ken early in my career, and one time I asked him how he became so successful. I expected to hear some wisdom that I could follow in my own career. Something like, "I sent out 5,000 promotional postcards a week," or "I read a book that had all of the secret steps behind being a successful performer."

Instead, he told me, "I guess I've just been around for a long time."

What?? That didn't bode well for my dreams of overnight success. I was confused, but he was kind enough to elaborate.

"You see when I started there were lots of comedians out there that had much more talent than me, but after one bad show, they quit. And they hardly ever prepared. If I had a bad show, I just kept moving forward. Over time I've worked on my craft and I continue to work on it."

So, there were steps to becoming a success, but they weren't so secret.

Preparation - Spending the time to work & plan ahead.

Perspiration - Committing to work on your craft.

Dedication - Moving forward, even when you feel like quitting.

No matter what your dream is, these three steps are key to achieving success!

TIP: Prepare, commit, and dedicate yourself, and success will eventually be yours.

Success Building Tip 5

THE PURSUIT OF HAPPINESS

All my life, I've loved to fish. I think it's safe to say that fish fear me. (Well, fish fear everyone, but still.)

When I was a kid, I was taught to drop anchor at my special fishing hole and wait for the fish to bite. That fishing hole produced a lot of fish, so I named it "Lucky Fishing Hole," even though I've done plenty of sitting there and other lucky fishing holes with little luck at all.

As I got older, I learned to troll for fish. It's a more aggressive form of fishing, where you move from place to place to find the fish. When you get a bite, you stay there for a while and enjoy the catching. When the biting is done, you move on. It's an attitude of, "Fish, I know you're in there, and I'm-a coming to git you!"

In life, I've found that finding happiness is like fishing. For a lot of us, we sit at our Lucky Happiness Hole, waiting for happiness to just fall out of the sky (or come up out of the water). Some days, we get a bite; others, nothing. Or we go back to places where we've experienced happiness in hopes of finding it again. However, happiness can be slippery as a fish, and waiting around just isn't enough. You need to proactive, looking for new people, places, and experiences. What brought me happiness yesterday may not make me happy today.

The Declaration of Independence says that all people have the right to pursue happiness. Even back then, our Founding Fathers knew that happiness was something that one had to go after. I bet they were pretty good fishermen, too!

TIP: Don't wait around for happiness; pursue it!

Success Building Tip 6

THE SEARCH FOR ANSWERS

The object of a question is to obtain information that matters to us. - Finding Forrester

A teacher once told me that there is no such thing as a stupid question. I totally agree, but then again, I've asked some weird questions in my day. Like time the flight attendant asked me if I had any questions about sitting in the emergency exit seat. Of course, I did! "What kind of antibiotics should I take if I've been bitten by a monkey?" (Bananacillin, obviously.)

When it comes to asking questions, the asking part is easy - easy enough that my little girls can do it. They ask questions all the time. I mean, ALL the time. The hard work comes when it's time to find the answer. That's the prize, and every answer has the potential to open your mind to a new part of the world you've never seen or known.

Look at all the cool stuff that makes our lives easier and fun and amazing; it all began with a question. Where would we be if Henry Ford didn't ask, "I wonder if I could make this cart move without being pulled by a horse?" Or what if the Wright Brothers were content with staying on the ground and didn't ask, "Can we make this bike fly if we give it wings?"

And I don't even want to imagine life without Martin Cooper. God, thank you for MARTIN COOPER! It was Mr. Cooper who wondered if we could make calls anywhere, moving the phone out of your house and into your pocket. Yeah, he invented cell phones! Then later on someone blessed us by answering the question, "Can this phone play music?" and then "Can it take a picture?" and then "How loud can it ring in the middle of church?"

There's no such thing as a dumb question. But it would be dumb to waste a great question by not looking for the answer. Start seeking the answer, and that's when the magic happens.

TIP: Learn more about the world by seeking out the answers to your questions.

Success Building Tip 7

LEARNING IS WAITING

"Some people will never learn anything because they understand everything too soon." – Alexander Pope

One great thing about being an adult is that I can buy more toys than I ever could as a kid! No more waiting for Christmas. No more waiting for my birthday. No more waiting to see if Mom noticed that I slipped a bucket of LEGOs into the shopping cart when she wasn't looking.

But believe it or not, waiting is not a bad thing, especially when it comes to learning something new. It would be nice if we could just plug our brains into a computer and learn new skills, like on The Matrix. My third lesson would be: "How to Instantly Play Classical Piano." (First would be "How to Start a Rabbit Farm," followed by "How to Sell Rabbits in Bulk on eBay," of course.)

However, we have to learn things the old-fashioned way, and I like that. There's a joy that comes with finding out you have a talent at something and that you can get better. The sad thing is, I see more and more young people who want to skip all of that excitement. They want to become the expert, NOW.

Every so often, someone will ask me about art, and I'm happy to take a moment to teach them something. But when I start teaching, they become like a broken record, repeating "I know, I know," and then start finishing my sentences for me! It leaves me wondering why they even asked in the first place if they know so much.

Today, be teachable! A big part of being teachable is being patient. You're not going to learn everything just in Lesson 1, so take your time and build your knowledge slowly. It's more likely to stay in your brain that way.

There's no rush. Unless you want to send me a bucket of LEGOs. In that case, use overnight shipping!

TIP: Be patient and teachable.

Success Building Tip 8

LEARN WITHOUT FAILING FIRST

Good judgment comes from experience, and often experience comes from bad judgment. - Rita Mae Brown, author

Do you ever think about those unfortunate souls who discovered all the stuff that you shouldn't do? Like that first caveman who realized you can't just jump out of a tree and fly like a bird? Or that first explorer who tried to ride a tiger like a horse?

Despite all of the lessons humans have learned the hard way, I'll admit to making some bad judgments. Many people, not just ones with ADHD, tend to see something and just go for it. They forget that just because something looks good doesn't mean it's good for you. Porcupines look cute, but you sure don't want to pet them.

In life we'll all make mistakes. Those mistakes are opportunities to learn and possibly make Good Judgment calls in the future. Learning from your mistakes is good, but I think it's even wiser to learn from the mistakes of others. Take a hint from bad judgments that other people made so you can avoid getting the bumps and bruises yourself.

Here are a few things I learned the hard way:

1. Six garbage bags do not make a parachute.
2. Giving your big brother a wedgie in his sleep is not a good thing.
3. Talking without thinking is never going to end well.
4. Be slow to criticize; the world does not revolve around you.
5. The golden rule is golden for a reason.
6. Doing squats in jean shorts is bad.

I'd be happy to go back and learn these lessons from someone else's stories. It would've saved me a tons of Band-Aids and at least one pair of jean shorts!

TIP: Be wiser and more open to learn from others.

Success Building Tip 9

ACTIONS HAVE THEIR OWN LANGUAGE

Well done is better than well said. - Benjamin Franklin

I haven't seen the movie that won this year's Oscar for Best Picture, but I KNOW I could've written the dialogue in my sleep! And I know that because The Artist is a silent movie, which means just what you might think it means: no talking, just acting. That's amazing to me, that the actors had to tell the story and captivate the audience just by their actions and expressions.

We live in a time when words are at the center of everything. Being that I am a speaker, blogger, Facebooker, and YouTuber, I seek to find the right words to say or write. Words are powerful, but actions can mean a whole lot more.

Several years ago, I had to hire an assistant to help keep my scattered ADHD brain from being so scattered. I set up interviews with several people, and I was shocked at how many of them didn't show up. At first I thought it was me. Did

I have the date or time wrong? I know I took my ADHD meds. But it wasn't me; people just didn't show up, and they didn't even call to cancel! One time, I talked to a person an hour before the interview, and he was still a no-show.

If you don't do what you say you'll do, people will learn not to trust you. That's no fun. However, if you follow up your words with actions, you'll find that people will trust and respect you. That opens up opportunities for cool relationships and friendships.

Doing what you say is a win-win for everyone. Actions really do speak louder than words.

TIP: Don't let your words be empty.

Success Building Tip 10

FULL SPEED AHEAD

In my travels, I rent cars pretty often. Every time I pick up a car, the sales rep asks me, "Do you want the gas option?" Normally, when you usually rent a car, you have to bring it back with a full gas tank. Otherwise, they charge you big-time to refill the tank. With the gas option, you pay for a full tank of gas at the beginning, and you just return the car at the end without having to fill up.

Sometimes the rep will give me the hard sell on the gas option: "If you buy gas yourself, it will cost you $3.65 per gallon. But it you take the gas option, it will only cost $3.45 per gallon. What a deal! Come on, it's a no-brainer!"

But what I have to remember is that I'm paying for a full tank of gas even if I only use half of it. The only way this is a good deal is if I return my car by coasting into the parking lot, driving on fumes!

At the end of my life, I want to be like that rental car. I don't mean changing my name to

Ben Honda and sticking a GPS to my forehead. I mean that I want to be coasting in on fumes, nothing left in the tank!

I want to have reached all of my potential, with all my dreams fulfilled and all my goals checked off. I want the Big Sales Rep in the Sky to say, “Ben, you lived life to the fullest.”

If you want to go out on empty like I do, here’s the key: Keep the pedal to the metal.

Keep moving forward. Rest when you need rest, play when you feel playful, but keep your engine running and never quit. The final parking lot comes around before you know it!

TIP: Keep moving!

Success Building Tip 11

WORDS, PART 1: THE POWER

Growing up, I wanted to be a magician. How awesome would it be to yell 'Abracadabra' and pull a rabbit out of my hat? The best I could get was a squirrel. (Where else was I supposed to keep my acorn collection?) When magicians use them, words like 'Abracadabra!' and 'Presto Change-o!' seem to have special power. But magicians aren't the only ones who use words with special power; we all do. The words we say have the power to change the people around us, for better or for worse.

It's a beautiful thing when we can use words to encourage each other. When a teacher or boss congratulates you on a job well done, it can set you in a good mood for the rest of the day. Kind words can help lift a friend's spirits when they're sad. And doesn't it put you on Cloud Nine when that special someone calls you their "lovey dovey shnookie wookums?" (And those aren't even real words!)

Unfortunately, whether it's teasing or yelling or gossiping, we know that words have the power to hurt, too. And we might not even realize that our words are hurting others. Like if you tell someone that their shoes are ugly, you might think that throwing in a "Just kidding!" makes it alright – but it doesn't. When you say something mean, the damage is done, no matter how many 'just kiddings' or 'not reallys' you tack on at the end.

Try lifting someone up with kind words and encouragement. It's an amazing magic trick, and it works every time!

TIP: Remember that words have power. Use them wisely!

Success Building Tip 12

WORDS, PART 2: THINK BEFORE YOU SPEAK

I love my feet. Thanks to my feet, I can run and jump and swim...and dance to my favorite Justin Bieber tunes. And without them, I don't know what I'd do with all the shoes in my closet! I'm really happy with my feet, but there's only one problem: They taste terrible!

Okay, so I've never taken a licking to my feet, but I have put my foot in my mouth on more than one occasion. What I thought would be a wise and witty contribution to the conversation ended up falling flat, maybe even hurting someone's feelings.

I love how the British writer Dorothy Nevill put it: "The real art of conversation is not only to say the right thing at the right place, but to leave unsaid the wrong thing at the tempting moment."

The "wrong thing at the tempting moment" could be a dirty joke in front of people you're trying to impress, or a sarcastic comeback when you feel like you're being criticized, or a gossipy comment about someone who just left the room. And sometimes as soon as the words leave your mouth, you regret it. You wish you could grab them in mid-air before they reach anyone's ears, but Wil E. Coyote has better luck catching the Road Runner. And he never catches the Road Runner.

The good news is that there's something you can do for "foot-in-mouth" disease: Think before you speak. Instead of spitting out that snappy comment that popped up in your brain, hold it there for a second. Weigh what you're about to say. How's it going to make people feel? Does it really represent who you are? Is it something you'd be ashamed of if everyone found out what you said?

It sounds like a long process, but it just takes a moment, and that moment can save you a lot of grief by stopping you from saying something you might regret. Unless you like the taste of toe jam. (Ew...)

TIP: Think before you speak and save yourself a world of trouble.

Success Building Tip 13

WORDS, PART 3: THINK BEFORE YOU TWEET

Yesterday's motto was 'Think Before You Speak', but in today's high-tech world, there are plenty of ways that we communicate. And with that comes plenty of ways to put your foot in your mouth. Or would that be "put your foot on your thumbs?" "Put your phone in your mouth?"

Thanks to the Internet and cell phones, we can talk to each other anywhere and anytime. How did I even survive before I could tell the world what my dog ate for breakfast?? (Which may or may not have been my favorite left shoe.)

It's exciting to think of all the new opportunities to share our thoughts, but it's kind of scary, too! Because when you're online, what you say there, stays there. Once you send that mean email or text in the heat of the moment, it's out of your hands. You just handed out a written record of something you might have regretted immediately.

Now more than ever, we need to think before we text, and think before we email, and think before we Facebook and tweet and YouTube. Of course, I thought about what I would say before writing this. If I didn't, I'd probably go on some tangent about buying a circus elephant off of eBay. (By the way, does anyone know where I can get a good deal on 200 pounds of peanuts?)

Keep those thumbs and fingers under control. As the saying goes, the Internet is forever, and that's a long time to have a mistake floating around!

TIP: Think before you "tweet!"

Success Building Tip 14

LISTEN!

Greek philosopher Epictetus said, "We have two ears and one mouth so that we can listen twice as much as we speak." I'm not a biologist or language expert, but that quote makes a lot of sense to me. It also makes sense that we have two hands and one nose so we can fist bump twice as much as we nose bump.

We've been talking about the power of words and how you can use that power responsibly when you speak. But unless you're the Energizer Bunny, there HAS to be a time when you stop talking and listen. (And since the Energizer Bunny doesn't talk, he must be an AWESOME listener!)

Listening isn't just taking a five-second break from telling your friend why vampires make better prom dates than werewolves. Listening has a number of benefits for both you and the lucky person you happen to be discussing supernatural cuties with.

First of all, listening just gives your brain and

mouth a rest. If you're like me, once you get started talking on a subject, it can be easy to go down a rabbit hole of twists and tangents, kind of like Alice in Wonderland. And the next thing you know, the Mad Hatter will be pouring you a cup of hot tea, but sometimes I'd rather have a bottle of iced tea, or maybe some cold Gatorade, like the kind they dumped on the coach in the last Super Bowl... See, there I go!

It's better to share my thoughts and then let my friend share theirs, which leads to the next benefit: Showing encouragement to your friend. Listening to someone shows that you're interested in them and that you value what they think. It shows them that they matter to you.

Finally, listening helps you learn new things. Think about school: the teacher speaks, you listen, you learn. Well, any conversation is an opportunity to learn something new – and you probably won't be tested on it later!

TIP: Listen to others and learn more about life.

Success Building Tip 15

THE COURAGE TO SAY NO

Have the courage to say no. Have the courage to face the truth. Do the right thing because it is right. These are the magic keys to living your life with integrity. – W. Clement Stone, author

A farmer once asked his two sons to help him plant the fields. One son agreed to help, and the other said no. For weeks, the son that agreed to help talked about how he was going to do it. He had a plan and and a slogan, and he even put the slogan on a T-shirt! But weeks went by, and he never went out to plant, not even a seed.

Meanwhile, the son who first said no felt convicted about it, so he decided to help out after all. He rushed out and started planting the field.

Which one of the two sons truly helped his father? Maybe the first brother didn't know how to garden, but just said yes to be nice. Maybe he felt pressured. In the end, it was worse for him to say yes because his father expected his help but never got it.

Let your "yes" be a yes and your "no" be a no. Too often people get stuck in the middle. It's like the "Maybe" option in those online invitations. If I'm hosting an event and you tell me "Maybe," that doesn't really help me at all! Will Papa John's let me order 5 pizzas and 2 "maybe" pizzas for all the people who will maybe show up? Give me an answer and stick to it!

If you're actually not sure, then just tell me that you need some time to decide. Take time and consider your decision before giving a confirmed 'yes' or 'no.'
It's okay to say 'no' as long as you really mean it. It even takes some courage. And it's a whole lot better than a 'yes' that you can't go through with, because there's no such thing as a 'maybe' pizza!

TIP: Let your yes be a yes and your no be a no.

Success Building Tip 16

THE INNER VOICE, PART 1: SELF-AWARENESS

I've seen it a dozen times on cop shows and movies: They arrest a guy with crazy hair and a funny look in his eye, and he tells them, "I hear voices in my head..." The cops think he's crazy, but I'm not so sure – because we ALL hear voices in our heads! The difference is, the voice I'm talking about is your own voice. (If you're hearing Kermit the Frog instead, you might want to get that checked out).

Have you ever wondered where self-confidence comes from? It's that inner voice saying, "Yes! You can handle this. You're unstoppable. Bring it on, baby!" And what about low self-esteem? It's that inner voice again: "No! You can't do this! You're unattractive, unpopular, and people don't like you. QUIT!"

So, your inner voice says two very different things at different times. Just like the things we say out loud, it's wrong sometimes, and you should ignore it. But since you've been hearing the inner voice your whole life, you might just accept what it says every time. Doing that will make your life as rocky as a roller coaster.

The key is to examine your line of thinking. Ask yourself "Why do I feel so down today?" or "Why am I telling myself I'm not good?" And on the good days, you can wonder, "Wow, I feel unstoppable! Why do I feel this way? How can I bottle that and drink it everyday?" This is self-awareness - a way of closely looking at your thoughts to learn something about yourself.

Becoming more self-aware will help you choose when to listen to your inner voice and when to ignore it. And if it tells you to sit on lily pads and eat flies, you definitely should ignore it!

TIP: Become more-self aware to better hear the inner voice.

Success Building Tip 17

THE INNER VOICE, PART 2: DEFEND YOURSELF

There was once a boring fellow named Harold Crick who led a boring life. That is, until a voice started booming out of nowhere, explaining his thoughts and actions as they happened. That would freak me out, and Harold felt the same way.

At one point, Harold felt stressed and worn out, and sure enough, the voice explained, "Harold suddenly found himself beleaguered and exasperated." As a strict and disciplined worker for the IRS, he responded with a simple "SHUT UP!"

You might recognize Harold and that scene from the movie Stranger than Fiction. I think the scene gives us great insight into the inner voice. Sometimes when the inner voice barges in, we need to aggressively take charge. It's like if a mean dog starts growling at you, and the survival instinct kicks in. You prepare to protect yourself because you never know what might happen.

Because we've grown to trust our inner voice,

we fail to defend ourselves when that voice is negative or abusive. It may tell us that we're worthless or not good at anything; that's an attack. When that happens, we need stand our ground and claim greater control over our thoughts.

The key is to fortify our defenses and protect ourselves. To do this, I have a unique task for you that may take some time, but it's an effective way to start defending yourself.

I want you to write yourself a letter of recommendation – not a resume, but a letter that highlights your strengths and accomplishments. What are you good at? What do people like about you? What do you like about yourself? What have you achieved that you're proud of? Nothing is too small or insignificant to put in your letter of recommendation. There should be no negativity whatsoever.

It's an uplifting letter that helps you to see the incredible person you truly are. And believe me, it does a lot more good than a simple "SHUT UP!" Happy writing!

TIP: Take the time to write yourself a recommendation letter. You'll thank yourself!

Success Building Tip 18

THE INNER VOICE, PART 3: POSITIVE THINKING

In a commercial for Dove (the beauty products, not the ice cream bars), a woman shows up to a photo studio with matted-down hair and the complexion of a Papa John's pizza. Then the team gets started like a NASCAR pit crew. The makeup artist turns the pizza face into porcelain. The hair stylist makes the nappy hair shiny and beautiful. Someone checks her tire pressure (or not).

The photographer starts snapping. The pictures are stunning, but they still get edited with Photoshop. The woman's neck is stretched out, wrinkles are removed, and her eyes are blown up to look like a Walt Disney cartoon. Supposedly, she now has "perfect" beauty.

This is a good lesson for dealing with the inner voice. As we said, the inner voice can be positive or negative. It all depends on which one has the greatest amount of fuel. Positive thinking is fueled from positive experiences, positive feedback, positive reading, and positive people. We choose to bring these things into our lives.

Negative thinking finds its fuel in different ways, but a big one is comparing ourselves to others. We usually do this without realizing it. We get so wrapped up in what others have that we forget our own gifts, like beating ourselves up because we don't look like someone in a magazine.

The kicker about the Dove commercial is that the "perfect" picture is plastered on a billboard. Everyday, men and women will see that billboard. Men will wonder why more women don't look like that, and women will be discouraged because they can't live up to the made-up example of beauty. It's The Lie, that perfect beauty exists and that you can attain it when it's actually not even real.

With positivity to drive it, the inner voice will guide you with encouragement throughout the day. Now that's a thing of beauty!

TIP: Bring positive things into your life to fuel positive thinking.

Success Building Tip 19

THE INNER VOICE, PART 4: BE CONTENT

Everybody is a genius. But if you judge a fish by its ability to climb a tree, it will spend its whole life believing that it is stupid. – Albert Einstein

I totally agree with Albert E. here. If you spent a year watching your fish, making notes of his progress in tree climbing, and making him feel bad about falling short, your fish would feel pretty stupid. You probably would, too. Of course, what Albert is getting at is that fish are simply not made to climb trees. That's not what they're supposed to do, so why in the world would they be judged on how well they do it? It's crazy that people do that to themselves all the time.

A perfect example is The Lie of "perfect beauty" that we talked about last time. People see the billboards and movies and magazines, and might compare themselves to those heavily edited and distorted images. We beat ourselves up for not being who we were made to be.

Americans spend over $3 billion in diet pills, $40 billion on research, and $50 billion on cosmetics! And if that's not enough, they spend $13 billion on cosmetic surgeries – as in going to a doctor's office and saying, "Can you take a knife and cut up my nose to look like this?" Or "Can you take my face and stretch it all over to take the wrinkles out?" (It sounds more like a horror movie than a medical procedure.)

A billion is a difficult number to comprehend, but one advertising agency did a good job of putting that figure into perspective. Consider that a billion seconds ago, it was 1959. A billion minutes ago, Jesus was walking around. A billion hours ago, our ancestors were living in the Stone Age. And it doesn't matter how much money people spend, how many pills they take, what procedures they have – it's never enough for them.

Why do some people find it so difficult to be content with being themselves? It's frustrating, discouraging, and depressing. The only solution is to stop judging ourselves for not being someone else. We need to be happy and content in being who God made us to be! I'm not saying that we shouldn't strive to learn new things and improve ourselves, but we first have to accept ourselves before moving forward.

So, let the fish swim, be yourself, and start climbing toward something better!

TIP: Stop believing The Lie; be content with who you are!

Success Building Tip 20

CONFIDENCE AND FOCUS

When I was in the seventh grade, I had a basketball coach that never missed a shot. It was amazing! From the free throw line - swish! A three-pointer - swish! And if by some chance the ball didn't go in, it was because of a gust of wind, or somebody moved the basket, or the gravitational pull of the moon. But by no means was it ever HIS fault when he missed a shot.

Around mid-season, the coach gave me some one-on-one shooting lessons, and I was dying to know about his perfect shooting record. I asked, "Why is that if you shoot the ball and miss, it's never your fault?"

He was happy to explain. "When I shoot the ball and believe that I have the ability to make every shot - because I believe I've made every shot - then I'm shooting the ball with confidence," he said.

Practice is important because it trains your body to find the right technique to shooting. But I think confidence is the key to success on the basketball court, and just about anywhere else.

If I believed that I missed a shot because I'm a bad shooter, then my confidence goes down. I'd focus on how many shots I've missed, and then think of myself as a disappointment. Then I'd develop a constant fear of missing shots, which would just make me miss more shots. It's a vicious cycle.

Confidence is a finicky thing. I don't think you're born with it, but rather it grows as you focus on your goal. We all fail at some point: we miss the shot, fail the test, or mess up on the job. If you focus on your failures, then you're robbing yourself of confidence and lowering your chance of success.

You should give only enough attention to your failures to learn from them and get better. Then, focus on opportunities and your potential for success.

TIP: Fix your focus, and confidence will follow. It's a slam dunk!

Success Building Tip 21

THE PROBLEM WITH GOOD INTENTIONS, PART 1

When I lived in Chicago, I drove by a homeless man everyday. He always sat on the same bench at the edge of a supermarket parking lot. He was tad older, and he rode around on an adult-sized tricycle with a trailer hooked to the back. In the trailer, he stored all of his treasures from mastering the art of dumpster diving.

When I passed him by, I would always come up with great ideas of how I could do something to help. I did this for almost three months and even starting sharing them with my wife. Maybe I could get him some toiletries, or maybe a jacket and some socks? How about a rotisserie chicken and a case of paper towels? Who doesn't like a rotisserie chicken? Juicy, perfectly roasted to a golden brown... (Mental note: Go buy rotisserie chicken for dinner.)

But I never did anything. I had good ideas, but they got lost in my busy schedule. I had plenty of excuses for why I didn't act on these ideas: "I'm just one guy; how much of a difference can

I really make?" Or "I go on mission trips, so I'm covered." And "This really isn't a good time; I'll do it tomorrow." Those are some great excuses!

I had good intentions, but good intentions don't make a difference. Actions do.

I'm an impulsive guy. It's part of the package when you have ADHD. For the most part, being impulsive for the most part is a bad thing, especially when it comes to metal objects and outlets. But this situation taught me something: We should never hesitate to act on the impulse to do something kind.

When reading this, you might start to feel guilty about missed opportunities in your past. May I make this subtle suggestion: DON'T FEEL GUILTY! This isn't about dwelling on the past. I want this to be a nudge to take action when those random moments come up in the future.

Amazing things can take place when you act on a good intention. I did, and next time I'll tell you what happened!

TIP: Never hesitate to act on the impulse to do something kind.

Success Building Tip 22

THE PROBLEM WITH GOOD INTENTIONS, PART 2

There was a cold, steady rain during the night of my birthday party, but that was okay. I got all kinds of good stuff, including some really cool LEGOs! My wife was driving, and I was inspecting my trove of goodies, when we passed my homeless buddy on his usual bench. He was covered with 50 blankets, just getting hammered with rain.

I instantly looked over at my wife and shared another brilliant idea on how we could help this guy. "We should get him a tent! Or some rain gear, or a slicker!" I didn't know what a slicker was, but it sounded fun.

While I was rambling, my wife suddenly whipped the car around. I thought we were hydroplaning to our deaths, all for my homeless buddy to see – at least he was getting a good show – but she was doing this on purpose!

I was squeezing the "I'm about to die" handle on our car ceiling when she pulled up right behind the guy. He was standing, staring into our headlights, probably thinking about running for his life. Then my wife said, "Get out."

"What? You mean all by myself?" I said.

"You have that huge umbrella in the back. If you care, give him your umbrella," she said.

"You mean by myself?!" I checked.

Of course she meant by myself, and that was the nudge I was talking about yesterday. She told me to back up my words with some action, so I did.

I got out in the rain with the huge umbrella, more like a tent on a stick. I opened it, but I opened it too far and had to wrestle it back into a usable shape. The guy started laughing at me. I finally gave him the umbrella and said, "I thought you might need this."

I was cold and soaking wet when I got back in the car, but I was feeling great. I don't know how much the umbrella helped the guy, but it helped me. It helped me to be on the lookout for those random moments when I could do something good.

TIP: One of your goals should always be "Be blessed by being a blessing."

Success Building Tip 23

YOU'RE SUPER, BUT YOU CAN STILL GET SICK

It's fun that I can see the comic book superheroes from my childhood in their own movies now. I can watch them run faster than a speeding bullet or swing from building to building on the big screen. But you know what wouldn't be fun to watch? Two hours of Superman laying in bed coughing with a fever and the chills. Superheroes can do just about anything, except get sick. It's too bad that we can!

I hate being sick, but the irony is that I tend to push myself to do things that make my sickness last longer. Instead of resting, I might go out and play or force myself to finish a project.

When we're sick, our bodies need special attention, and we need to listen. Here's my list of recommendations for when you get sick.

1. Get lots of rest. Most of us stay up late and get up early, so our sleep bank is running on empty. This is the perfect time to load up the bank.

2. Catch up on your reading. We live in an ADHD world where our time for reading is limited to Twitter-sized captions. Who has time for a 250-page book? You do, if you're sick.

3. Eat comfort food. Too many of us are microwave maniacs, so take the time to make some chicken noodle soup and a grilled cheese sandwich. Better yet, have your friend do it while you stay curled up in bed!

4. Receive love. This a great opportunity for the people around you to love on you. Don't rob them of the blessing, and enjoy the attention.

5. Get better quick. There's a good chance that you've infected your whole household, so you'll soon be the one making soup and sandwiches!

Being healthy is like its own superpower, so don't take it for granted. Fight off sickness and get back to saving the world!

TIP: When you get sick, interrupt your routine and do what it takes to get better.

Success Building Tip 

WHAT TO DO ON A BAD DAY

The sun'll come out, tomorrow. Bet your bottom dollar that tomorrow there'll be sun! – Little Orphan Annie

I was sick recently, and it wasn't a good day, but it wasn't horrible either. I got better, so how much do I really have to complain about? It wasn't too long ago that a day like that would have ruined me. When I was feeling down, I'd have the tendency to see only the bad. Then I'd start thinking about what I thought was wrong with my life, ignoring everything that was so good about it.

If you have to make a major decision, I recommend NOT making it when you're down in the dumps, because you can't get a clear picture of your life. Otherwise you might show up wearing clown shoes to your sister's wedding, and take it from me, you do NOT want to do that.

Be cautious of the mind's ability to go on a downward spiral. So many things need to be considered before we take a nosedive into a pool of negativity. Here's a good checklist for the next time you're feeling down.

1. Why are you feeling this way? Even though this seems like an obvious thing to ask, so many don't.
2. How much sleep did you have the night before?
3. When was the last time you ate? Hunger can be a distraction without us realizing it.
4. When was the last time you overdid it eating? It's possible to have too much of a good thing.
5. When was the last time you got good exercise? Exercise is positive fuel for the brain.
6. Are you sick?
7. Or are you just feeling a bit off today? Everyone has them.

A bad day shouldn't derail you from what you're doing, and it shouldn't make you forget all that you've accomplished. Tomorrow is a new day, and the chances are good that there'll be sun!

TIP: Don't give a bad day more attention than it deserves.

Success Building Tip 25

A MENU OF CHOICES

When I was a kid, my family's menu at home consisted of two choices: Take It or Leave It. Now that I'm older, it's nice to go to a restaurant have some options.

Wouldn't it be nice if life was like that? You stroll in, get a menu with colorful pictures and descriptions, and someone is there to explain everything to you. Then you order: "Yes, I'll have the baby back ribs, and my sides will be an order of success, and a helping of wealth, and... does happiness cost extra? 99 cents? Okay, I'll have that."

However, life doesn't have a simple, laminated menu with smears of barbecue sauce. Our choices aren't spelled out so easily, and a lot of people are left not knowing what they really want. When you tell the server, "I just need a couple more minutes to decide," a few years go by.

You end up looking around and settling for what everyone else is having.

"I'll have what he's having. Oh, that's the uncertainty with sauteed hopelessness? Hmm, I don't know...hopelessness gives me gas."

Life offers so many choices, it can be overwhelming. But the great thing is that you always have the choice to change yourself. It's not that if you make the wrong choice, you're stuck with it forever. You can choose to learn new things by reading more or taking a class. It's your choice to take up new hobbies or make new friends. For some of you, the best choice might be to pick up and move for a fresh start.

On today's menu, the special is...well, I don't know! You're the chef; choose something good!

TIP: Make your own choices, and don't worry about what everyone else is having.

Success Building Tip 

HOW TO DREAM, PART 1: THE PRICE

I was about to speak to a group of eighth graders about careers when I saw a poster on the wall that said, "Dreams are Free." In a way, I thought there should have been this fine print at the bottom to clarify it: "But there's a cost if you want them to come true."

These days, it seems like many people don't take their dreams seriously. It's as if we've been conditioned to dismiss a dream even before considering its potential or the steps to reach it. The word "dream" itself is mostly used to describe things that are unrealistic and pointless.

If we find the courage to get to the second stage of a dream, which is to share it with others to get an outside perspective, we often preface it with, "I know this sounds like a stupid idea," or "Don't make fun of me but I think..." We already believe that our dreams are not realistic before they have a chance to get off the ground.

I want you to challenge you if you've been treating your dreams this way. Here's a simple project to help you understand your dreams.

1. Make a list of your top dreams. Like "Become a doctor," "Travel to Australia," or "Learn to play the guitar."
2. Put a checkmark next to any dreams you've started to pursue.
3. If you can't make any checks, think of the reasons why you haven't started pursuing your dreams. Write them down.

Sometimes our mind tricks us into thinking these reasons much bigger than they really are. Seeing them written down might show you that they're not as big of a roadblock as you thought.

Okay, poster, you may be right. Dreams are free. But what's the point of free dreams if they're not meant to come true?

TIP: To see a dream come true, you have to be willing to pay a price.

Success Building Tip 27

HOW TO DREAM, PART 2: TRUE DREAMS

Introducing the new iPhone 7Gx3! It texts, tweets, takes photos, washes your dog, bakes muffins, removes nail polish, and calls your mom before she complains that you don't call home anymore! Only $200! (Requires a $2,000 a month contract.)

I wouldn't be surprised to see this commercial in the next few years. You know you'll want one, but that $2,000 per month isn't growing on trees. So, you'll need to decide if you're willing to do the work to make the money. How badly do you want that phone? (Depends on how badly your dog smells, I bet.)

Dreams are kind of the same way. It comes down to asking yourself one question: How badly do I really want it?

Are you willing to do what it takes to make your dream come true? Would you get up two hours early to work on your book? Would you endure the pain of running and working out to make the team? Would you skip the fun party to concentrate on your work?

When you ask yourself these questions, it may turn out that you're not willing to work that hard or give up that much to make your dream come true. And that's fine! What you thought was a dream might be only a fun diversion. It's much better to know this before you're neck deep in it.

Do you have that list of dreams you made last time? (If not, then you might need to clean your room; it's only been a day!) Take that list and cross off that fun diversion and move on to the next dream. Ask yourself how badly you really want this one. And keep going down the list.

What will be left on your list will be your true dreams. These are the things worth your time, effort, and energy. And the iPhone 7GX3 shouldn't be one of them. I'll loan you my phone for only $1,000 a month!

TIP: Your true dreams are the ones you're willing to sacrifice for.

Success Building Tip 

HOW TO DREAM, PART 3: FAILURE

He was a sophomore in high school when he tried out for the varsity basketball team, but he didn't make it. The next year, he could have skipped tryouts out of fear of not making the team again. Instead, he didn't let a fear of failure stop him. He made the team and ended up becoming the greatest basketball player the world has ever seen.

Of course, I'm talking about: me! Just kidding, it's Michael Jordan! You know, the guy who's on all of the shoes?

In my life, I've seen that the fear of failure may be the biggest obstacle to achieving one's dream. I've certainly worried about it. What if I do all of that hard work and make all of those sacrifices just to fail in the end? It almost makes you not want to get out of bed in the morning.

But failure doesn't have to be a bad thing, as crazy as that sounds. Thomas Edison said, "I am not discouraged because every wrong attempt discarded is another step forward." Edison tried many different materials before he found the right one for his light bulb. Each failure was one step closer to finding the right answer.

I love Michael Jordan's commercial where he talks about his failures. He's missed over 9,000 shots, lost 300 games, had 26 times to win the game and missed. Then he sums it up: "I've failed over and over and over again. That is why I succeed." I believe he took those misses and lost games and learned to become a winner.

Failures are going to happen. Instead of letting them stop you, use your failures to make you better.

TIP: Failure might be what you need to get closer to reaching your dream.

Success Building Tip 29

HOW TO DREAM, PART 4: POTHOLES

Have you ever been driving down the road when all of a sudden, PA-ROOM! and the car rattles. A pothole. Potholes are little obstacles in the road that make you drive more tentatively.

The road to reaching your dream has potholes, too. These obstacles can frustrate you, slow you down, and make your life harder than it needs to be. And they take some of the fun away from pursuing your dream.

Here are a few examples of these obstacles and what you can do to avoid them.

POTHOLE: Too many things to work on at one time.

SOLUTION: Narrow it down. My ADHD, hyper-drive brain has 1.47 gazillion ideas bouncing around. But pursuing too many things at once can just leave you with lots of beginnings and no results. Focus on one task at a time, get it done, and move on to the next one.

POTHOLE: You need to take a big risk to move ahead.

SOLUTION: Take it! To make money in the stock market, you have to take a risk and invest some money. To win the game, you have to take a shot that you might miss. The biggest rewards come at a risk.

POTHOLE: Too much work for you to handle.

SOLUTION: Involve other people. You can't do it by yourself. Your book needs someone to edit it. Your music needs someone to spread the word. Getting others to join your dream is the only way to capture it. And encouragement from others is the best fuel to keep a dream alive.

Watching for potholes and making adjustments will keep your ride smooth!

TIP: Don't let potholes slow you down. Solve the problems and keep going.

Success Building Tip 30

EXPERIENCE IS WHAT YOU MAKE OF IT

Experience is not what happens to a man. It is what a man does with what happens to him. - Aldous Huxley

When I was in the 10th grade, I reached my maximum height of 6 feet, 4 inches - and I was the runt of the family. My older brother was 6'7, and my younger brother passed me at 6'5. However, our dad was a mere 6'2. We come from a long line of sasquatches.

We were out driving one evening when we pulled into a gas station. We'd only been stopped for a few seconds when someone slammed into the back of our car. We were all a little shocked when this guy got out of his car and started screaming at my dad for committing the heinous crime of being parked in a gas station next to a gas pump.

My dad calmly got out of our car to handle the situation, but this guy was looking for a debate that would end with him pummeling my father into the ground. When the guy started poking my father in the chest, the brothers and I decided to see if Dear Old Dad needed any assistance.

Just like out of a movie, our three doors opened at the same time and we three Sasquatch Juniors stepped out. It's amazing how fast this man changed his mind about what type of experience he wanted to have that night.

He learned quickly that we ultimately have a choice in how we handle the not-so-pleasant experiences in life. Patience, wisdom, kindness, and compassion are examples of positive character qualities that we can draw upon when things seem to be going wrong about us. Keep them in mind, because that car you bumped just might be full of sasquatches!

TIP: Experience is a choice; choose wisely!

NOTES

NOTES

Looking for an inspiring and fun speaker for your next teacher or student event?

Consider Ben Glenn, The Simple ADHD Expert! A full time speaker since 1994, Ben's teacher and student presentations are filled with great stories and life wisdom that help inspire, motivate and change attitudes. Ben's presentations are as useful as they are entertaining.

Reviews of Ben's presentations:

"Ben, WOW! I was really moved by your appearance today. As a first grade teacher and a mother of a son with ADHD, your show gave me lots to think about. I always wanted to present my son's ADHD as an opportunity. You gave me the proof! I will look for future opportunities to see you, and someday want my son to see you as well. Thank you for all you are doing."

SUZIE B.
Teacher & Parent

"Ben gave the audience more than I can ever describe. The words you read here - no matter the outstanding accolade, no matter the lofty praise - can't adequately assess the reaction from our group of future educators. Quite simply, Ben changed attitudes about working with children with special needs, he reinforced each attendees' desire to educate well, and he encouraged the spirit of all. He dazzled and entertained. If your goal is to have a successful event, you won't make a better choice than Ben Glenn."

AMANDA GRAHAM
Director, Future Educators of America

"Ben Glenn was incredible!! I was at the FEA National Conference as a teacher with my FEA students. On an evening when they were tired and may not have paid much attention otherwise, they were totally enthralled with Ben's art and message. I loved watching their faces, rapt with attention. How wonderful. :-) We thoroughly enjoyed the entire thing!"

NANCY S.
Teacher

For more information about Ben's presentations, please visit, SimpleADHD.com

Follow Ben on:

 @simpleadhdxpert

 @simplybenglenn

@simplybenglenn